Your Simple Path

Find Happiness in every step

like that! I know that might sound a little crazy but it's true.It's as if the energy, the healing energy inside the book lifts me instantly.

I keep this special little book very close. Depression had control over me for many years, but whilst reading Your Simple Path I began simplifying my life and it has helped me enormously.

Your Simple Path

Path

Find Happiness in every step

Ian Tucker

BOOKS

Winchester, UK
Washington, USA

First published by O-Books, 2014
O-Books is an imprint of John Hunt Publishing Ltd., Laurel House, Station Approach,
Alresford, Hants, SO24 9JH, UK
office1@jhpbooks.net
www.johnhuntpublishing.com

For distributor details and how to order please visit the 'Ordering' section on our website.

Text copyright: Ian Tucker 2013

ISBN: 978 1 78279 349 6

A CIP catalogue record for this book is available from the British Library.

Design: Stuart Davies

Printed and bound by CPI Group (UK) Ltd, Croydon, CR0 4YY

We operate a distinctive and ethical publishing philosophy in all
areas of our business, from our global network of authors to
production and worldwide distribution.

Contents

For Serena, Jacob, Eve and Alfie.

Foreword

I first met Ian when my son started to play for the local under eights soccer team.

Ian was the coach but of a kind very different from those of the other teams we played.

Some of these men would rant and rave and criticise – and, on occasions, reduce some poor little lad to tears.

Ian, by contrast, was quiet, gentle and positive. He was always supportive of every player in the team, whatever mistake he might have made.

In their pre-match and half-time huddles, the boys would sit around him, leaning in to hear him, and would absorb every word he uttered. They trusted, respected and loved him. Thus inspired, the team rarely lost and became the best in the region.

When he showed me an early draft of Your Simple Path it was clear that this same, gentle understanding and wisdom was there for all of us.

Ian Tucker is one of those rare people who seem to know about who we really are and how easy it is, in a frantic world, to forget and become lost.

In the last few years, my family has been through some dark places.

My wife and I nearly died from eating poisonous mushrooms which wiped out our kidneys and put us on dialysis for four years.

The impact on us all was severe.

It was sometimes hard to stay positive and not to wallow in a swamp of self-pity, bitterness and guilt.

Ian's simple words of guidance were a source of strength.

I know this book will do the same for all those fortunate enough to read it.

Nicholas Evans,
International best selling author of *The Horse Whisperer.*

"Love's Whisper ..."

There comes a time in everyone's life when a gentle
light begins to shine within, a calling for you to
realise what really matters.

How making others laugh makes you laugh more,
how reducing others' fear makes your
own disappear.

How being grateful for the little things brings even
bigger things to you.

And that how peaceful you are is the true measure
of success.

Have you heard "Love's Whisper" yet?

Life

Life – it's a simple word. In essence it's the period between birth and death, most of us get about eighty years at it and are generally provided with everything that we need to have a good time.

They even tell us that the best things in life are free and so on paper we have it made.

Common sense would suggest that if we spend eighty years doing something we'd become pretty good at it, but for some reason that doesn't seem the case with Life.

As you read this book you're living your life.

How's it going? No, seriously, how's it going?

You'll be a certain age in a particular place and by now you will have a title or label that defines you. It tells others how important you are, or if indeed they should interact with you at all.

Doctor for example is deemed to be a particularly good one, whereas bank manager doesn't carry as much clout as it used to.

At some point we have decided that a politician is more important than a lollipop lady; that we should respect a managing director more than the people who keep the building clean and house husband still doesn't roll off the tongue as easy as housewife.

Outside of your title you may be a Miss who wants to be a Mrs., or a Mr. who wants to be a Miss.

At this very moment you could be relaxing on a sofa, dug in on a battlefield, commuting on a packed train or waiting on death row, either way, this is the life that you have chosen.

Some of you will be able, but decide not to move, whilst others will be disabled and live life on the go.

Initially you wanted to be older but now you're not getting any younger.

There's a very good chance that you want to look different to how you think you look and you may have even spent money on picking the perfect nose.

Most of us will be happy when, but when never seems to come.

Perhaps you will find happiness through the next purchase, the next win, the next deal, the next lover – the clue's in the word next.

You will often choose to live with regret rather than put it right in a heartbeat.

You'll be judged throughout your life, how you look, the colour of your skin, how you dress, how you dance (if you dance), how you smile or how you don't.

People will make a decision on you before you have even spoken to them and if your accent doesn't fit they'll judge you on that too.

This of course works both ways and your constant comparison and assessment of others brings with it a lifetime of fear-based criticism, jealousy and insecurity.

Relationships will have come and gone, each time followed by relief or heartbreak and now you could be single and longing for someone or married and craving solitude or someone else.

You live in a world that works day and night to make you just like everyone else. So fit in. Wear this. Eat that. Shape up and do as the others do.

It seems that Society has a plan for all of us and you have a part to play, but why is it so rarely the part that you would have chosen for yourself?

Winning is everything although we pretend it's the taking part that counts.

Competitive parents stand and scream at sporting seven-year-olds desperate for them to beat other seven-year-olds, as life's lessons are passed down a generation so they can fit in too.

Children offer us one of the rare chances in life to truly make a difference and yet we choose to pile on all the pressures that we too felt at that age, even though we may now believe that there is more to life than grades, medals and finishing first.

Money makes the world go round, so hopefully you have some, but if you do there's a likelihood that you earn it in a job you don't want as reducing your debt takes over from living your dreams.

Your perceived success will be based around what you have. The house, the car, the clothes, the friends, but the people it attracts will reduce in line with your bank balance.

However long your life, you'll count the people who stuck around regardless on the fingers of one hand.

There's an increasing probability that the illness that stops your life will be caused by stress, and most of the stress in your life will be caused by trying to be the person that others believe you should be.

Nothing drains your energy like not being true to who you are.

A quick fix is available and normally addictive, prescription or otherwise, they soften the blow and get you through.

Religion may be another option for you but depending on where you are in the world your life may be in danger if you choose the wrong God.

Indeed, even as I write countries are at war to make sure their God wins.

Life moves on quickly and there's a tipping point that takes you from ambition to regret as "If only" becomes your bedfellow.

As you reach society's take on old age the clock on the mantlepiece begins to sound like a countdown, and our ultimate fear, death, stops being something that only happens to other people.

For many it will also be time to assess how you have lived your life.

What were the moments that really mattered and did you make the most of them?

Did you simply exist and react to your life or could you have made more of a difference?

Have you lived the life that you wanted for yourself, or the one others expected of you?

Ultimately, perhaps the most poignant reflection will be:

What was your life for?

What was your purpose?

What was the meaning of your life?

Do you take care of me?

I'd like you to take a moment to reflect on your life to this point.

To help you, picture yourself as a little boy or girl on your first day at school.

If you have one available then a photograph at this age works perfectly.

It's important for you to know that however many years have passed, whatever has happened to you in your life, you are the same person as you were on that first day at school. There is a part of you that has never changed.

You will have met thousands of people and experienced many things and all will have shaped you into the person that you are today, but you can still feel an instant connection with the small child that you are now beginning to visualise.

Take a few deep breaths and if it helps close your eyes.

Start by picturing your face, your soft delicate skin, look how bright your eyes are, you may have teeth missing which only magnifies your charm. Does a fringe or pony tail add to your crowning glory?

If you were wearing a uniform then what colour was it? How do you remember feeling as you sit in your classroom on your first day? Who else is in the classroom with you? Can you remember their names?

Can you now associate a smell with the image? Soap? Clean hair? (Well, it was your first day).

Perhaps you relate the smell to your mother or whoever held your hand in the playground or maybe something else, freshly cut grass, floor varnish, paint, glue, school dinners.

Can you recall your teacher? What was his or her name and how do they look?

What about sounds that you associate with your first day at

school? The school bell, excited classroom chatter, laughter, nursery rhymes or music playing?

Now sense your energy at that age, innocent and carefree or perhaps you were apprehensive and feeling nervous.

Begin to relive and feel how things were for you back then.

So, very quickly you have created a wonderful scene and can now see yourself sitting amongst your new friends on your first day of school. You have called upon all of your senses to complete the picture.

I would now like you to imagine that the "adult you" is standing just outside the classroom looking in through the window. You can sense that the energy in the room is one of pure anticipation and wonder at all that can be achieved in life.

You just know that the "little you" whether nervous and shy or excited and outgoing feels that anything is possible, and indeed probable. As you look around the classroom all of your tiny friends feel just the same way.

It is now the end of your first day at school and through the window you can see that everyone apart from you has left the class.

You watch as "little you" packs your bag and misbuttons your coat.

Suddenly they look up and you both smile exactly the same smile.

As you walk slowly into the classroom little you sits down and you take the small chair next to them.

Little you reaches for your hand and looks up into your eyes, you will know exactly how they are feeling.

"How am I?" they ask nervously.

"Pardon?"

"How am I?" they repeat, a picture of innocence. "Do you take care of me?"

"What do you mean?" you ask, a little taken back.

"Do you take care of me? Am I ok? Am I happy?"

"Well, sometimes you are, but life's hard and it makes it difficult to be happy."

"Why is it difficult? Isn't being happy the most important thing?"

"It's just not that easy, we become very busy with more important things, oh and other people don't always help, extra money would be good, our bodies can sometimes let us down ... "

Now you're on a roll. "Also you never know what life will throw at you next. Just as you think you have it sorted something happens and you're back to square one, it can make you feel so helpless."

They look puzzled "Yes, but I can still be happy can't I?"

"I'm afraid it doesn't work like that," you reply, running out of answers.

Their little hand tightens in yours.

"Ok. Then am I kind?" they enquire, their voice is a little more timid now.

"Well, you try to be but again it's not always possible to be kind."

"Why not?"

"For the same reasons that you can't be happy!"

You become conscious that unfortunately your words of wisdom are beginning to sink in, but before you can change the subject little you continues ...

"But the golden rules seem really easy don't they?"

"What golden rules?" you ask.

"The golden rules that we learnt in class today, the teacher told us that they would help us to have a happy time."

"What, you mean at school?"

"Yes, but she also said to us that even though they are only simple we can use them for the rest of our life, so did we?"

"I'm sorry, I don't remember them," you reply.

"Well, they are called the five golden rules and if we get up and work on them every day then our time will be worthwhile, what does worthwhile mean?"

"It's good, it means that your time here won't be wasted, why don't you remind me of what the teacher told us and I'll tell you how we are doing."

Do you take care of me?

Just for today.

Were you honest?

Did you worry about things?

Were you kind to everyone that you met?

Have you lost your temper and got angry with people?

Did you remember what you already have in life to make you happy?

So, how are you doing? Are you taking care of yourself?

The five golden rules will make as much sense to you now as it would have on your first day of school. It's obvious that if we saw them as daily tick boxes and managed to mark them each evening we would be in a much better place.

Total honesty, no worries, kindness in abundance, calm and peaceful and all wrapped in an ability to count your blessings?

Who wouldn't sign up?

Of course, as you answer them and read on you'll want to raise the fact that at five years old real life hadn't kicked in.

The opening chapter of this book gave you all the excuses you need to dismiss the previous page as ideological but not practical.

Life exhausts us, it sucks us in, spins us round and spits us out. It's mad, it's manic, it's crazy.

It's noisy. It never stops. It's relentless. We are too busy holding on for dear life for checklists.

How can we be truthful in a world that lies to us?

Can we really be asked not to worry when surrounded by so much uncertainty?

Can we show kindness even to those who make it difficult?

Can we risk being seen as weak and roll over when showing our temper would keep others in check?

Isn't it only natural to want more?

If only there were a way ...

Meaning

Christmas Eve and I sit alone.

It's almost midnight, my wife and three young children are all in bed, the presents are wrapped, the turkey and trimmings chilled and ready to go.

I pour another glass of red wine and settle down in front of the TV to watch a congregation sing carols by candlelight.

The words as ever seem to resonate with me and everyone sings badly like they only get to do it once a year.

Following the madness of the Christmas build up this hour or so alone had become a sort of tradition for me each year.

An acknowledgment that the queuing, the pushing and shoving, the no parking, the panic buying, the card writing, and the once a year family visits had all come to an end. A realisation that for now there really is nothing more that can be done.

Christmas seems to be one of those times of year that lends itself to reflection, to stopping for a moment to think about how our life is going. What have we achieved? How we are not getting any younger and are we getting it right?

Luckily for me I was, and my career was far exceeding my expectations.

I was working in sales and personally responsible for managing a £30 million business whilst directing over one hundred people, my earning potential was uncapped and meant that myself and my family could enjoy a very comfortable lifestyle with all that comes with it, and all before the big Four Zero.

Only that afternoon my boss had called to say how delighted the shareholders and American owners were with our end of year performance. They wanted to congratulate us again for year on year improvement in a difficult market.

So, bonus in the bag, praise in abundance and every career box ticked, all I needed to do now was quietly join in singing "Little Donkey" and finish off the mince pie and glass of milk that had been left on top of the fireplace for you know who.

So why on earth would I suddenly get the feeling to give it up, to simply walk away from everything that I had ever been certain I wanted to achieve in my life? This wasn't about some five year life plan. Within fifteen minutes I knew that for some reason I was never going to be the same person again. Thoughts of uncertainty were replaced by a knowing that everything was perfect and a gentle quiet confidence grew out of limiting beliefs that I could only ever be the person I had created or that others recognised as me.

I felt the need to write something down, maybe just to confirm what I had experienced. This was completely out of character for me. I found myself with pen and paper in hand staring at a blank page. I was now sitting in complete silence and felt very much at ease and there seemed to be a calm, peaceful energy to the room. After a few minutes the words "Love's Whisper" came to me. I wrote them down in speech marks at the top of the page.

What then began to flow from the pen brought tears, and just a few lines that seem so obvious and yet elude so many offered me the chance to reconnect with something more meaningful in life and reassess what really mattered.

I have since read that the psychiatrist Carl Jung compares our lives to a typical day, he talks about the "morning and afternoon" of our lives. In the morning our values focus on career progression, material gain, status, wealth and obtaining more. But he suggests that at some point there is a subtle but definite shift and we step "thoroughly unprepared into the afternoon of our lives" to begin a search for something more, something that gives meaning to why we are really here.

And there's no "typical" age for this to occur. Everyone walks their perfect path at just the right time, and as we arrive at this particular turning we just need to make a decision on which way to go.

I guess as I sat there that evening my life clock had just turned midday.

For most people this internal shift or calling does little more than create questions or uncertainty about how their lives have evolved. Are they happy? Is this it? The intensity begins to disappear and is often dressed up as "oh, he had a midlife crisis" or "she just went off the rails for a while but she's ok again now."

But for some, indeed a growing number, the seed has been planted and simply choosing to ignore this inner calling is not an option.

So what happens when so many of the things that seemed important to you lose their significance? Or you realise that having more, or the promotion, or the best or the latest or the prettiest or the fastest doesn't hold the same value and certainly doesn't guarantee happiness.

What happens when you realise that there's so much more to life than the job title, or the house that you live in, or the car that you drive, or the clothes that you wear, or even what other people think of you (especially what other people think of you).

Well, it leaves a void, a space inside of us that may have been filled before with a certain train of thought or set of values. But when you hear "Love's Whisper" or step into the afternoon of your life, you just know it's time, it's your time, for fear to be replaced by love (even if at this point we are not sure what love really means).

Initially this can seem disorientating or confusing. We would have been told by society and even those who love and only want what's best for us, that we needed to live and be a certain way; that we needed to fit in.

That the morning of our life "checklist" is the way to go. Get ahead, stay ahead, get more, earn more, have more. Not just to keep up with the Jones's but to get the next model up, and then you'll be ok, you'll be happy.

So, midlife crisis or new life beginning? Have you fallen out of society or fallen into who you really are? Are you trapped without answers or liberated to create your own?

How can we truly find meaning and develop a life that brings us joy and happiness whilst offering us a calm, peaceful outlook?

For me it began a journey of discovery. And for the past ten years or so I have read countless books that promised answers as well as books that left me with even more questions, I've listened to spiritual masters as well as everyday people who have an angle or a view on how it should be.

I've sourced and watched thousands of hours of footage, retreated for periods in total silence, tried chanting for answers, and come to know the absolute benefit of meditation and quietening the mind.

Out of all of this a pattern began to emerge, a thread that in some way has linked my decade of discovery to not only the main religious and philosophical theories and teachings but also to a straightforward daily approach that brings ancient wisdom to our crazy modern age.

And like so many things that work perfectly in life there is a real simplicity to what I now know will offer us true meaning.

A number of simple principles and if we get up each morning and work on them they will improve our lives beyond belief.

The following pages will begin to introduce them to you. It is, however, important for you to realise that if it all seems a bit too simple or obvious you haven't missed a trick.

You see, we all know life's true meaning, we were born with every answer we will ever need. But shortly after, the "world" took over, and suffocated our true and natural ability to be happy and at peace.

It's now just a matter of stripping away the layers of things that we have been told mean everything, so that we can once again reconnect with what will really bring us Joy, Peace and Happiness.

Now is all there is ...

"Even after the longest winter, spring is sure
to follow."

"Now is all there is …"

Religious and philosophical text has always told us that "living in the moment" is the true path to sustained inner peace and happiness, but is this practical with today's busy lives? We have to make plans for the family or work, juggle our time and divide our attention across many areas. All of which seemingly takes us further away from the present moment.

Being more conscious of living and being happy and content in the moment doesn't mean that we never plan or structure our day, week or month. In fact it's important to have things to look forward to as long as we don't become too reliant upon them.

In the same way it's healthy to reminisce and think about what has gone before. We just need to remember that it's how we look back that's important.

Being present simply reminds us that we are living our life right now.

"Worry"

As you read this, does your happiness depend on something that may or may not happen in the future? If so, you are basing your peace of mind on absolute uncertainty, not a great platform or foundation for inner peace. It begins to sound like a lottery and we all know the odds on a lottery win!

Worrying is like praying for something you don't want.

My father once told me that almost everything that he had ever worried about had never happened. It's not just my dad who realises the futility of worrying about the future. Ghandi told us "There is nothing that wastes the body like worry."

How many times have you worried yourself, sometimes to the point of illness, about a certain situation and it never happened?

How many times have you said or thought, "I had nothing to worry about" because the outcome was perfect?

On nearly every occasion that we are uncertain or anxious about the future, the outcome is nothing like we thought it would be and actually turns out much better.

Quite often we even end up relieved that things didn't progress as we had hoped. There have been many occasions when I was desperate for a particular outcome only in hindsight to give thanks for a completely different conclusion.

But by that point, how many "moments" have you lost never to get them back? How many times have you not given someone who you love and care for your time and attention? Or your mood (and theirs) has been affected because you are worrying about something that just isn't going to happen and is taking you away from this moment.

"Regret"

If we begin to accept that worry and anxiety over future events take us further away from how we really want to feel, then what about regret or disappointment for something that has already happened? Something that has gone forever, in fact something that doesn't even exist anymore.

Any amount of money or focus can't change what has already happened. The only place it now resides is in our mind. So in essence it is entirely up to us how we allow a past event or situation to make us feel.

It's now nothing more than a memory, a wispy illusion where the storyline, characters and plot change and move depending on how we want to remember it at any particular point.

There are two ways out of any single thought. But only one of them usually serves our best interests, and yet very often it's not the one we choose.

But just like worrying about the future, regret or living in the past has a massive effect on our ability to be happy now, to truly be free to live our lives.

This is beautifully wrapped in a verse from American author Barbara De Angelis: "The more anger towards the past you carry in your heart, the less capable you are of loving in the present."

So when you think of something that has already happened and has gone forever, do you allow it to hang heavy? Or are you able to liberate yourself by remembering the cherished memories or experience gained and move on?

Can you learn to recognise that in your bigger life picture almost every event carries very little significance in how you can truly feel at any one time?

"Give or Take ..."

"There is no better exercise for your heart than reaching down and helping to lift someone up."

"Give or take ..."

After recognising that the current moment is all you can ever truly rely on, let us now look at what will offer you the next step along Your Simple Path.

Regret and worry are just two of the emotions that we can feel at any time. Our emotions are our feelings, they give us an indication of how we are doing, how things are affecting us.

Unlike our thought process which at times can play tricks on us, our emotions really do serve our best interests. They are a true indication of how we really are. We can be dishonest, we can even train our mind to believe a certain story, but deep down, inside, our emotions always let us know what's really going on.

It's important to realise that one emotion exists to create another. How can we feel happiness without first knowing sadness? Recognise the blessing of being cared for if at some point we have not felt lonely? It's healthy for us to acknowledge that we need our full range of emotions to grow and evolve.

Inner peace and happiness will not be found within some sort of clinical existence where nothing ever goes wrong. We will have things come into our lives that test us and it's at times like this that we are given the chance to realise how alive we really are.

We come into our own not only in the sunshine but also in the eye of the storm.

Another way of looking at it is if there were only left and no right, then we would have to go the long way round every time!

Our emotional well-being is closely linked to another part of our make-up, our behaviour and actions.

How we act or interact with our self and others also has an absolute bearing on our outlook towards life.

Our emotions and actions are directly connected. For example, if we act a certain way it will have a direct effect on how we are feeling.

If we saw a stranger who obviously needed our help and we offered it, then that would create an appropriate emotional reaction. On some level we would nurture a caring or kind feeling. And in turn the stranger would respond with feelings such as gratitude and appreciation.

But if we were to attack or harm that person then emotions such as aggression or hate would emerge and create fear and anxiety within them.

Our actions at any one time also have lasting effects on our ability to be happy.

For example, helping the stranger will serve our best interests moving forward. We will develop positive and cherished memories, which will in turn create a warm and endearing emotional response. We can even call on that occasion if we are in need of simply feeling a bit better about ourselves at some point.

In contrast, what if we had chosen to verbally or even physically harm that person? What do we carry with us? Regret? Remorse? Guilt? Anxiety?

And in the other person perhaps revenge? Anger? Or even aggression back towards you or another?

Every action creates a reaction and not only within ourselves. Even more apparent, when we allow ourselves to think about the effect it has on the other person.

There is a very good chance that a kind act from you would leave them wanting to reciprocate in some way, either with you or another.

So even without knowing it you have created a chain reaction of good will, your simple act moves forward into a world that is in desperate need of someone just like you.

A kind gesture or word from you has a wonderfully uplifting effect on others. In today's society interaction and unconditional kindness can often be scarce, but something that seems nothing to you can change another's life.

A smile to a stranger who had given up hope of anyone smiling at them ever again. A hug for someone who just needs to feel wanted. A reassuring arm around the little boy or girl who's not the team's star player ...

You have a choice with every action. You have a fabulous opportunity to look after not only your own mental and emotional state but send ripples of happiness out into the world to touch the hearts of everyone.

The following illustration takes just a small selection of our full range of emotions and actions that are available to all of us and places them on a simple template.

Anything below the line would perhaps be less welcome than those placed above.

Happy   Forgiving   Compassionate

Empathetic   Generous   Calm   Honest

Complimentary   Caring   Allowing

Grateful   Respectful   Authentic

Kind   Loving   Sympathetic

Worried   Aggressive   Violent   Revengeful

Depressed   Dishonest   Guilty   Selfish

Insecure   Fearful   Anxious   Lonely

Controlling   Critical   Complain

Manipulative   Rage

Take a moment and review the example.

Every one of us will have experienced all the emotions and actions shown and there's a very good chance they will all be a part of our lives again, even if only for a moment or in a much more conscious state.

I think it's safe to assume that we would all wish to spend more time above the line; it's simply a more inspiring, peaceful and joyous place to be.

What if I told you that above the line is who you REALLY are and that you have simply created what appears below as a result of falling in line with a collective consciousness.

You live in a world that recognises below the line as normal, you spend every day with people and newspapers and television channels that encourage you to stay down there.

Each night a national news summary on every major channel, spends half an hour feeding fear to millions without taking any responsibility for finding a solution (that's if the issue even exists in the first place).

Occasionally they will include a 30-second "light at the end of the tunnel" snippet but then straight back to the major damning headlines to close the programme.

Strangers, work colleagues, even family will often question the authenticity of that rare individual who dares to choose happy and not sad or gratitude over complaint. "It's just not natural."

Is there a chance that you are being drawn to above the line because seeing it in this way reminds you of your true nature?

Well, let's look at what's natural. A bird wouldn't sing below the line. A tree couldn't root there. And that infectious laughter of a toddler would fall silent amongst "embarrassed and fearful" or "manipulative and deceitful."

So, if this is beginning to make sense to you on some level then how can we simplify it even further?

Take another look at the illustration. How would you summarise the two sections?

Some of us may look at one section as a positive outlook whilst the other is negative. Or maybe one is born out of love and the other fear and both would be perfect analogies.

Now look again, just a little deeper. Is there a pattern to the words on each side, regardless of whether they are actions or emotions?

These words carry a great life lesson. Words such as caring, sympathetic, complimentary, sincere, compassionate. The list could go on and on, but they all point towards the same thing.

To feel good, to be above the line and closer to your true authentic self, we should look at what we can do for others, whilst looking to develop an existence where bringing happiness and peace to others comes before our self.

A sense of concern for others gives our life meaning, it is at the root of all human happiness.

In the same way, below the line could be termed "What's in it for me?" As words such as complain, control, manipulate, revenge and anger all support the notion that we have to have it our way, that inner peace and happiness come from controlling an outcome, any outcome, in order for the end result to be just as we would like it.

Allow yourself a moment and begin to imagine your life if you could lose all the emotional baggage, the stress, anxiety and heartache associated with uncertainty and the need to be in control.

Sense the weight and heavy energy that goes with your negative or fearful emotions and actions lift from you, to be replaced by the lighter, peaceful more energetic vibrations that you feel when you begin to take yourself out of the equation.

Developing an outlook that puts others before yourself shouldn't just stop at people who you have come to know and even love. Imagine how your life would change if you could extend this to all living things.

At this point I would like to introduce you to a wonderfully inspiring concept and a perfect way to step out of your society-induced cycle of the need to control your life.

A very dear friend of mine Stuart Morris is the director of a Natural Health Centre in Birmingham, England.

When I was preparing to write this book he encouraged me to run a series of talks and very kindly offered me a room at his Centre. His advice and insight as ever proved to be perfect. The talks grew in popularity and as I was able to help others find their Simple Path in life their feedback and interaction within the group really began to shape and define the message further.

At the end of the first talk I went to him and asked how much I owed for the room hire, without hesitation he asked me to "pay it forward."

I must admit that I wasn't sure what he meant so enquired again. He asked me to think of an amount that I would expect to pay and give it to a stranger as a random act of kindness. This immediately made sense to me and I found myself excited but a little nervous about the whole thing.

When I pushed Stuart for who, where and when, he simply said "don't worry about that, you'll just know when the time is right."

The following week I was in Liskaerd, Cornwall. The family and I were walking back to catch the train when the heavens opened and it began to pour with rain. We took shelter in a charity shop that by any stretch of the imagination was a little down on its luck, bare shelves and not much else were on offer. The only other people in the shop were two female volunteers.

After spending a small amount on a couple of things we noticed that the rain had stopped and our train was almost due, so went on our way. As I left the shop I got an overwhelming feeling to go back in, Stuart's words of "you'll know when the time is right" became very prominent and so I asked my wife to carry on with the kids and I would catch them up.

When I re-entered the shop the lady at the counter asked if I had forgotten something? I enquired if she could tell me about the charity and her eyes lit up. With real enthusiasm she began to explain that it supported local adults with learning disabilities who were able to attend a creative day centre, and the proceeds from the shop paid for the materials required.

As she was explaining I took the money from my wallet. I found myself so full of gratitude that I had been given the chance to actually connect with this lady and handed her a donation.

Both of them became very emotional and told me that was typically what the small shop took in a week – and that's when the hugs started.

I told them that it was a gift from a very special place in Birmingham and congratulated them on the inspiring work that they both do.

So by recognising that the actions and emotions associated with giving rather than receiving always sit above the line, it is possible to consider "paying it forward" rather than the need to always "get something back."

Perhaps we then begin to understand the wise and knowing words of His Holiness the 14th Dalai Lama.

"If you contribute to other people's happiness, you will find the true goal, the true meaning of life."

"What goes around ..."

"Give as you wish to live."

"What goes around ..."

Initially you may be sceptical about your main focus being on bringing happiness to others. After all, we have spent our lives believing that we need more not less. To win not lose. To gain not give. These have been our lessons as we search for happiness ourselves and now we are being asked to give it away.

It could be perceived by many as a sign of weakness. How could you possibly just keep giving? It's exhausting. It's just not right. And surely the more we give, the more people just take, take, take.

What happens when we have nothing more to give? What about if WE need more? Is it just like a bank account and at some point we're empty with no overdraft facility?

Ok, so here's the clever part. Remember, for every action there's a reaction.

This planet that we all call home needs to balance, it turns on its axis every day. Occasionally there is a manifestation that we often call a "natural disaster" such as a volcano erupting, or a tsunami or hurricane that devastates an area. It may be that if no lives are lost we can recognise them as wondrous, majestic acts of nature and the earth's ability to explode with raw, untamed beauty.

In contrast, every day and at almost any time we all have the opportunity to witness our earth's ability to be still, or tranquil. It's all around us, but we are just too "busy" most of the time to notice.

A soft mist as it lies against the surface of a lake. A gentle warm breeze as it caresses and slowly dances through long grass on a summer's day. A majestic oak tree that stands perfectly still and seems to have secrets to tell. A full moon on a quiet, clear night.

There is a knowing in nature that everything is in balance.

A tree doesn't grieve for falling leaves on an autumn day. It sheds its leaves to the soil in the knowledge that in giving and nourishing the ground around it, they will return.

It gives its fruit until it has no more, until to us it looks bare, but the tree knows the secret of the universe. Whilst it stands it has an unlimited abundance. Giving makes way for more.

In fact, giving at just the right time encourages growth.

Imagine the tree clinging for dear life to every brittle leaf and becoming ever more fearful and anxious because it thinks that it has no control over nature's flow.

Think about that for a moment. Leaves seem to dance on the wind as the tree waves farewell, full of gratitude that everything always turns out just right.

The Persian poet and philosopher Hafiz knew the same thousands of years ago when he observed "The sun never says to the earth you owe me – look what happens with a love like that, it lights up the sky."

So how is that relevant to us? Well, because we are an absolute part of this planet, of the universe. We breathe the same air, need the same light and share the same rainfall as every living thing.

Therefore, if we accept there is a natural balance on the planet, then why would it be any different for us?

Here's the key. We don't give to receive, but what we do give, we naturally get back.

It's what makes the world go round.

What goes around comes around. What you put in you get out. We've sort of heard this already. It seems to make sense to us. Perhaps now, for the first time, you are being asked to approach it from a deeper humane level.

It's not just about working longer hours gets you the promotion, or training harder gets you the gold, or more revision delivers a better mark (although they may do).

This law is as absolute as gravity, if you jump off a building, it doesn't matter how much money you have, how beautiful you are, what you have or haven't supposedly achieved in your life, you're going to fall and hit the ground.

The universe sings your song. If your lyrics include peaceful, kind, caring and happy, then it will line up like-minded people and opportunities to sing along with you.

If on the other hand your main verse contains words such as anger, anxiety, resentment and dishonesty then a queue will also form, as the world is full of individuals looking for someone with a song just like yours.

So your choice of actions and how you can bring happiness to others not only affects your ability to be happy, but also attracts the people, events and opportunities that come your way in life.

Looking at it this way it becomes obvious to us that only one song choice can deliver true happiness. It's now just a matter of deciding if you want to sing along.

In other words, like attracts like, and the reward of giving happiness to others is that just like the tree and its fruit, it will return to you and leave you in full bloom to give again and again.

"Letting go ..."

I'll be happy when, If only I hadn't, I feel desperate, I feel insecure, I'm sick with worry, I'm anxious, I'm out of control, I need to manipulate this, I'll complain, you owe me, I'll show you, I need more, I need less, you need more, you need less, What about me? I know best, how could you possibly know, now you listen to me, I'll never be able to, you'll never be able to, I can't face it, I don't want it, I'm desperate for it, you can't have it, I haven't got enough, I've got too much, I need you, you need me, I don't want you, why don't you want me, it's too hot, it's too cold, please don't rain, I haven't achieved, it's too late, it's too early, I need it now, I need to change, you need to change, we need to change, the world needs to change, it's not fair, that's not how I planned it, you never smile, you don't love me, what if I lose, I have to win, what will they think, what if I fail, I have to have it, I don't want you to have it, what if you die, what if they die,

What if I die?

"Letting go."

The pace and turmoil associated with modern life sweeps us along and lays down markers to how we are measuring up against everyone else. A constant review of perceived achievement or under-achievement. All day, every day. It exhausts us. How can we ever be at peace if our whole life is a competitive race against time and everyone else?

The pressure to conform, to be right, to be happy, to please everyone, to pay the mortgage, to look good, to be popular, for our kids to do better than we ever have, so they can be "happy."

All the above comes at a cost. It's called attachment. We have got ourselves into a cycle that suggests that our happiness and inner peace are dependent upon things outside of our control.

We become our job title, the car we drive, how we look, even the illness that killed our father or grandmother.

Every generation comes along and seems ever more reliant on outside influence, looking for other things to make them happy. Material wealth, electronic wizardry, faster, smaller, better, going further. But the irony is that these things take you away from what will truly deliver happiness.

Could you possibly detach yourself from things that others get anxious and worried about?

Release yourself from limiting beliefs that the only outcome can be the one that you want right now?

Can you begin to develop a gentle understanding that the less you attempt to control or manipulate a situation the more you allow a natural order to ease into your life?

Compare your approach to a flowing stream. As the water rolls down it creates a path. If there is a natural obstacle then it gently works its way around it and continues its journey. The energy within the water is always the same. But just like the tree that sheds its leaves, it knows that everything is perfect. Sometimes it's slow, other times it quickens, but perfect all the same. There is always a way through, and so it arrives clean and pure.

Now imagine a different stream, this time the water is desperate to reach the same desired destination. It stops, attempts to go back, becomes stagnant, smashes against anything in its way, breaks its banks and dissipates. The destination for both streams is exactly the same, which route do you take?

Whilst there is a passive element to this approach this in no way means that we relinquish our desire to reach a goal, or an end result.

A musician can write or learn a piece but understands that the performance becomes magical when they are able to let go and lose themselves within the music. I've heard it said that it's the space between the notes that makes the difference.

In writing this book, I approach each chapter with an outline, an intent, but have truly come to understand that when I relax, the right words appear on the page at just the right time.

The Tao Te Ching is a Chinese masterpiece that offers us a timeless guide to life.

The author Lao Tzu tells us: "When I let go of what I am, I become what I might be."

"Allow me to introduce Yourself ..."

"You are never alone."

"Allow me to introduce Yourself."

What if I told you that as you sit here reading this book you are not the person you think you are?

I know it's a strange concept. You were there at the birth, you've grown up with yourself, watched yourself physically change, you have got to know yourself really well.

If you put this book down and went and stood in front of a full-length mirror and looked, what would you see? Who stare's back at you? Your human form. But is there more to you than meets the eye?

You will quickly realise that there are parts of you that you cannot see, but that you know exist. Your thoughts, your emotions, they all make you who you are, yet are non physical.

Would you allow yourself to go a step further?

If you are willing to accept that you are more than just what you can see, then could there be even more to you?

You may have already experienced what I am beginning to describe and know it as your sixth sense or gut feeling, your instinct.

It's not tangible, you can't really explain it, but if you recall a situation when you have listened and trusted, then it will always have looked out for your best interests.

It cares for you, gently guides you, it contains your life purpose. It has every answer you will ever need. And as you begin to connect and deepen your relationship with it, treasures will be revealed to you that will change your life.

A single note within a piece of music that seems to touch you deeply. A flower moving gently on a summer breeze that makes perfect sense to you. The stillness of an ancient oak. The dawn chorus. This is who you really are, this is what your mother saw when she looked into your eyes as she held you for the first time.

Pure, kind, natural, giving.

This hidden part of you has many titles, especially with indigenous and tribal people who all recognise it as your true essence, a timeless part of you that connects you to the universe and eternity.

Typically in the West, words such as soul or spirit begin to create an understanding. You may have heard the terms higher, inner or true self. Although perhaps the more we try to label it the less we understand it.

On a recent Your Simple Path workshop, I asked the group to think about an analogy that could begin to help them understand their relationship with their true Self.

Here's a lovely example.

Imagine that a mother is at home with a toddler. They are both in the kitchen and Mummy is busy preparing the evening meal. Pans boil away, the oven is too hot to touch and knives and sharp implements are on show.

The little one is in no danger and plays with her toys at the other end of the room.

Even though all around her is potential harm, the presence of her caring mother makes her feel safe.

All is well whilst the little girl feels the protective and safe presence of her mother and she remains calm and happily goes on playing.

Now envisage the effect on the little girl if her mother had stepped outside and the door had locked shut behind her. Suddenly the little one senses the separation, now the pots could boil over, the oven is fire, the knives could fall.

Nothing has actually changed for the little girl apart from becoming detached from her source of comfort and love.

As she looks up at the window her mother smiles and gently whispers "open the door" and the little girl is calm again. All she had to remember was that she wasn't alone. As she opens the door her mother picks her up and holds her close.

This example uses pots, pans and knives to make the point but could easily be anxiety, stress and worry.

The key is separation from a part of you that sees the bigger picture and knows that everything is going to be ok.

If we look at the previous chart it defines our actions and emotions as above or below the line.

Anything below is typically associated with a lack of trust, the need to control, it comes from a part of us that we have created ourselves; it is called our ego.

To help you understand the relationship between your higher or true self and your ego I'd like you to imagine the birth of a child.

In the delivery suite, as the baby is born, uncertainty, anxiety and fear are replaced by sheer awe and amazement as the energy in the room changes and for a moment, just a moment, it all makes sense to us.

The newborn baby brings with it a pure, serene quality.

I remember that after all the noise and turmoil associated with the birth, that first moment of eye contact I had with my children caused my heart to melt. I sensed the total trust and faith that they had in me and all of life.

This may be the closest we get to both witnessing and understanding that higher or inner part of us, as both theirs and indeed ours, are on show.

It's not long, however, before a gentle shift takes place as "can't do" replaces "can do" and our "hopes" seemingly become "hopeless."

We all begin to construct a survival mechanism. It's called our ego, and every block we build takes us further away from who we really are, or even more important, who we could be.

Our ego keeps us in check; it reminds us to stay small. Our ego is fed by fear and is readily available with list after list of why you couldn't possibly live your dream or be with that person.

It darkens your natural light, attempts to silence your beautiful voice and would definitely rather you hadn't picked up this particular book.

So as you read on allow yourself to remain open as each page gently loosens your ego's grip and lets your true light shine through.

"A step at a time."

The sole purpose of this book is to ask you to consider what is really important to you in your life, what really matters?

While at the same time, helping you become fully aware that you can reclaim your life and begin to create a version that inspires you and others.

The first part of this book looks at a typical life. It may not be your life but there will be a thread to it that you can relate to. How we step onto life's conveyor belt and are then too busy holding on to truly enjoy the journey.

We then move on and begin to look for a meaningful purpose to all of this.

To simplify our outlook on life so that we can truly focus our energy towards something that nourishes that inner part of us. To find something that defines our happiness and well-being, whilst developing a positive platform for real change and liberation.

To help us further strip away unnecessary layers, we looked at just a few things which if we were to accept and introduce into our daily routine, would have a tremendous effect on our ability to find purpose and meaning.

Recognising that we can only ever find comfort and solace in the present moment is a massive first step towards taking back control of our lives. The past has gone forever and you have absolute control over the only place it now resides, your own mind.

Take care of yourself and let your memories bring you peace and not anguish.

Remember not to base your happiness or peace of mind on an event that may or may not happen in the future. It's good to have something to look forward to, but not if you let the outcome become so important to you that it takes you away from your right to be happy now.

Developing a conscious understanding that our behaviour or actions go a long way to determine our frame of mind or how we feel is the next step.

We have an absolute choice with every action, safe in the knowledge that choosing kindness brings us inner peace and happiness every time.

Once we remember that being kind, gentle and considerate is who we really are then we give it away. We serve others. We become selfless. We take ourselves out of the equation and stop asking "What's in it for me?"

As we give we get back. In fact what we give we get back. It's a self-fulfilling prophecy. So kindness meets kindness, anger results in anger, like attracts like and this is without exception.

So choosing your life and what you surround yourself with couldn't be easier, just give as you want to live.

Let go. Go with the flow. Trust, believe and have faith.

Remember you are getting back what you give out. The outcome will arrive at the perfect time.

The only bit you need to understand is that it may not be "your" version of the perfect time.

The person who until this moment you thought you were, is merely the tip of your iceberg.

Your physical form is nothing more than a vehicle, a set of clothes to step forward into the world. The real you, your true self, contains the wisdom of the ages.

It knows your story, your purpose for being here. It holds every answer and only ever wants to guide and protect you. So make friends with it and prepare to amaze yourself.

The second part of this book simplifies the approach even further, but brings the words off the page and into your life forever.

So, can you change?

Well, if you think change is worrying you should try the same old routine, it's lethal.

Now take a deep breath and step forward to claim back what is rightfully yours, a life of Joy, Peace and Happiness.

"Your Simple Path to Happiness."

I would like you to approach the second part of this book with an open mind, remember that your ego, that part of you that seeks to control you will throw up all sorts of barriers and reasons why your new-found approach to life isn't for you.

Very quickly you will be able to recognise this and separate yourself as limiting thoughts and beliefs are replaced by a lighter more vibrant and inspiring outlook on life.

There are four steps along Your Simple Path, they are in a logical order, but as you become familiar with them they can also be used individually as well as collectively.

You are invited to approach each section in the same way so you will quickly become accustomed to the format.

Each step begins with a mantra or passage, a simple message, just repeating this to yourself will have a tremendously positive effect on you.

Following an introduction there are a number of exercises that will help you to quickly build each step into your everyday life.

Although each one can be completed in minutes do not under-estimate how beneficial your time spent on each of them will prove.

Finally, the first three steps are each complimented by a guided meditation that can be found at **www.iantucker.co.uk**

Each one contains a beautifully inspiring piece of music called inner peace by Ajna. It has been specially adapted for each meditation and will relax you as I guide you through.

The good news is that you cannot get this wrong, it's all about your intent and what you would like to achieve.

Step 1

Forgiveness

Step 2

Gratitude

Step 3

Peace

Step 4

Freedom

Forgiveness

"To forgive is the highest, most beautiful
form of love.

In return you will receive untold Peace
and Happiness."

What is it about forgiveness that frightens us so much?

Why was this chapter the hardest for me to write?

I mean on paper it makes perfect sense. We are offered this wonderful ready-made solution to liberate ourselves from anything that has come to test us.

A proven method to smash the shackles that tie us to a certain someone who has hurt us or left us in pain.

Forgiveness sets us free. It gently unties the knot in our stomach that swells each time you think about a past event.

It allows you to step out in quiet confidence rather than live in avoidance.

It opens the curtains and lets sunshine bathe the room that would have remained in darkness.

Broken hearts are put back together piece by piece and left stronger than they were before.

We no longer need to feel imprisoned by mental and emotional attachment as forgiveness unlocks every door.

Forgiveness returns us to a place where inner peace and happiness dwell.

It offers a wonderful sense of relief and lifts a weight enabling us to travel light without the destructive mental and emotional baggage that we so often carry throughout our lives.

And yet even though we know its life-changing benefits, why are we so reluctant to forgive?

We'd rather sign up to living with debilitating emotions such as anger, resentment and jealousy than look to find peace through forgiveness.

Our hearts ache with unresolved feelings caused by issues that can stay with us for a lifetime.

And all because we can't say the "F word."

Our lack of forgiveness often harms us more than the person or issue itself.

We hang onto throw-away lines that can hurt our feelings for decades. Or take exception to someone's reaction just because they saw it differently to us.

We hold a grudge for something that we know deep down we too have done to others. We take exception to an action that we may have even considered ourselves under the circumstances.

Have you ever told a lie? Cheated on another? Not played to the rules and won? Stolen something? Used aggression? Been deceitful? Taken sides for convenience? Knowingly let someone down? Manipulated a situation for your own gain regardless of another's feelings?

Need I go on?

Have you ever been unable to forgive another for any of the above even in the knowledge that you act exactly the same?

This begins to help us see the frailty of clinging onto an action that is deemed wrong by us, simply because it belongs to someone else and yet expect others to accept it if we put our name to it.

There will of course be genuine reasons for us to feel aggrieved by another's actions. An unprovoked attack, a partner being unfaithful, our loved ones or those close to us harmed in some way. But even then, even when we see no way out, forgiveness offers us a lifeline and enables us to work gently through the situation in our own time whilst giving us a chance to move on with our lives.

It is important for us to understand that forgiveness never means condoning the action or behaviour that has hurt us, but allows us the prospect of not remaining a victim for life.

Maybe it's the religious "holier than thou" connotation that forgiveness carries with it. Perhaps we associate this ancient wisdom with those far more enlightened than us.

Forgiveness is a gift to you. It wasn't dreamt up because they were a couple of lines short in the Lord's Prayer. It's a natural process that restores our faith in life.

For those of you with young children, you will know that if they could read this they would laugh out loud at the absurdity of holding onto all this stuff. Forgiving to them is as natural as laughing out loud (something else we're not so good at as we used to be).

So, is it possible to re-introduce ourselves slowly to a belief that may be seen by many as weak in a world that demands strength? Or as letting the other person off the hook when we're encouraged to show them who's boss?

Real courage and strength lie in forgiveness, not in harbouring resentment or anger towards another.

Besides, by holding on and not looking to let go who really wins?

We remain attached to that person forever, a prisoner to the memory with all the additional heartache that has built up every time we've thought about it over the years.

There has to be a better way.

It is important for us first to acknowledge that forgiveness is a personal choice, and as such we should not and cannot rely on another person.

We can therefore take total responsibility for forgiving another or ourselves without the need for permission or anyone else's involvement.

This in itself is wonderfully liberating since all it takes for you to relieve yourself from the burden of past issues or the crippling pain of anxiety and fear is you.

There are only two types of forgiveness. We can forgive ourselves or we can forgive someone else. The principle of both is exactly the same but I would encourage you to begin with working on yourself.

As you begin to work on self-forgiveness it will enable you to detach yourself from limiting beliefs that you cannot move on with your life. It will show you that positive and inspiring change is not only possible but also a natural consequence of forgiveness.

Self-forgiveness offers you a perfect platform on which to build a foundation for inner peace.

It gives hope to what you thought was a lost cause, and gently wipes your slate clean, in order for you to take the experience and move on from it a better person.

Let us now look at forgiving others. You may feel that this is more difficult because there is someone else involved, perhaps someone who has hurt you in some way.

This is where we need to remind ourselves that we are not looking to condone behaviour in any way and that which has already gone before can't be changed. It was a moment in time now gone forever.

Our forgiveness of another will, however, remove our attachment to that past event. Enabling us to take the experience and lessons learnt without remaining suffocated by the negative feelings that we have associated with it.

So how can we begin to develop a forgiving outlook in everyday life?

Take a moment with the words of the Dalai Lama: "If you want others to be happy, practice compassion. If you want to be happy, practice compassion."

So what is compassion and why should it appear right in the middle of a chapter on developing forgiveness in your life?

Compassion is often associated with or even mistaken for empathy and sympathy.

Here is the difference between the three:

Empathy is acknowledging someone else's situation, empathy does not mean that you agree with or share what they are going through, it simply means that you understand it.

Sympathy means that not only do you understand it but that you feel exactly the same as they do about it.

Compassion takes both of them and makes you want to help. It says to the other person, I understand how you are feeling and I want to make it better for you. I want you to be free of suffering.

Compassion is kindness in its purest form, having compassion for someone lightens their load. Eases their pain, lets them know that they are not alone.

If you were to unravel your own compassion it would contain warmth, sincerity and sensitivity. It would be unconditional, tender and caring. And it would show you the true meaning of how to love yourself and others.

So why is compassion the key?

It enables you to approach forgiveness from a place of understanding.

It allows you to say to yourself or the other person "I recognise why you did this because I too have been there and I want to help."

Compassion reminds you that each person you meet has a peaceful, loving side and helps you to seek their innocence and not their guilt.

It ignites within you a loving, kind nature. And as we get back what we give out, it won't be long before your need to forgive subtly reduces and is replaced by a new peaceful outlook on life.

Dr. Wayne Dyer tells us "When you change the way you look at things, the things you look at change."

The next few pages will begin to build forgiveness into your everyday life.

It's at times like this that your ego, that part of you driven by fear and doubt, and the need to control, will throw up all sorts of reasons why you shouldn't have this book open at all.

I can almost hear it now "Well done you for sticking with the book this far, but can we PLEASE get back to what's in it for me? We're wasting precious worry time here!"

The good news is that the next few pages will start to create a subtle shift within you. It will help you identify with your true or higher self, recognise it as who you really are, and begin to isolate your ego's grip on how you feel and act each day.

In a short space of time you will even begin to recognise when your ego is attempting to block your route to a happier existence, but you will remain focused on what you know your correct course of action should be.

Before you begin, I would like to relate a poem by a Zen Master called Ryokan.

He was a Buddhist monk who lived in the early nineteenth century, famed for his simple, compassionate approach to life and his love of all people.

His poetry has gone on to make him a national hero in Japan and his work and presence inspire me greatly.

One of his poems offers these words of wisdom. Read it a couple of times and let it sink in.

If not for you, I would have counted to one hundred, to one thousand, and yet never come to understand what it means, but now each time I count to ten, ten times to make one hundred.

So how is all this relevant to developing forgiveness in your life?

Start simple. Don't let your ego look to prove you wrong.

Instead of attempting to count to one hundred, count to ten, ten times and achieve the same outcome.

Look to begin your forgiveness work on issues or people that won't test you too much; those niggly little things that hang around your mind but take up your time. We all have them but they add up.

Practise makes perfect and each time you are able to remove a layer of anxiety or a thread of regret your work is done and you can move on.

Ten little one's make a big one so go easy on yourself.

Finally, I would like to give you an account of something that happened to me.

Each week I join a group of friends for a game of football at a local indoor sports centre.

Although competitive, the emphasis is very much on enjoyment and trying to keep fit at an age where perhaps we should know better!

One week a man came along who I had never met before and played on the opposing team, after about five minutes we found ourselves running quickly side by side, and without warning he pushed me with both hands into the wall.

I put out my hands to protect myself and after hitting the wall at full speed and hearing the crack, I immediately knew that I had broken something, the pain in my right hand was severe.

Within an hour both hands had become very swollen, and as I lay in bed that evening feelings of anger and even revenge began to dominate how I was feeling. Who was this man? This stranger? Why had he shown no remorse? It was unprovoked. He had only met me a few minutes earlier.

The following day an X-ray confirmed that I had broken my hand, and would be in plaster for 6 weeks. At the time my job was dependent on my ability to drive, and so loss of earnings become a factor. It was early summer so I was unable to surf or play any sport with my children.

After six weeks the plaster was removed and another X-ray showed no signs of improvement, which meant another six weeks in a cast with the possibility of surgery at the end of it.

For over three months, a sudden, violent act from a stranger had come to really test me. The plaster cast, pain and inconvenience were a constant reminder of the incident, but above all they had created in me harmful thoughts and possible actions against another person.

Almost six months to the day and the town where I live had its Christmas carnival, the streets were full; music, dancing and festive cheer were all around. As I carried my son on my shoulders I turned a corner and bumped into someone coming the other way, I recognised him as the man who had broken my hand.

As he looked back at me I was able offer a genuine smile, any thoughts of revenge or hostility had disappeared and with no knot in the stomach or lump in the throat I wished him a Merry Christmas.

At that moment I realised that through the work that is about to be introduced to you I had been able to totally forgive him and move on.

It felt wonderful, almost magical.

I mentioned at the beginning that this chapter was the most challenging for me, but working through it and developing an active approach to forgiveness has had an amazingly positive effect on my well-being.

Now it's your turn.

"Developing Forgiveness in your everyday Life."

"Morning Kindness"

"Within your Heart"

"Evening Reflection"

"Morning Kindness"

Allow me to remind you that compassion is your ability to recognise and act when someone needs your help.

As you awake each morning you will have time to think about your day, perhaps only a few minutes but that is all this exercise will take.

I would like you to introduce a simple focus on compassion, on developing a caring nature towards yourself and others.

This should be a daily practice, so only focus on one day at a time.

Each morning use the following three affirmations (or even better develop your own).

Just for Today I will show a random act of kindness to a stranger and tell no one.

Just for Today I will look for opportunities to help another person unconditionally and expect nothing in return.

Just for Today I will go easy on my supposed faults choosing to focus instead on what I have done for others.

And that's it.

A gentle, quiet commitment to yourself and the universe each morning that seemingly takes you out of the equation and puts your focus on what you can give, rather than what you can take.

"Within your Heart"

This very simple but powerful exercise will give you the opportunity to forgive and free yourself from specific people or issues.

Please remember that forgiveness begins with your ability to forgive and show compassion towards yourself, and for this reason there are two exercises, one to work on self-forgiveness and the other to develop forgiveness towards others.

There needs to be a depth to your approach here, I suggest that you begin each session with the following:

Once you have chosen the person you wish to forgive, attempt to find something, however small or seemingly insignificant about them that reminds you that they are vulnerable, that just like you and I they make mistakes and sometimes we are simply a part of that mistake.

Now look to introduce the following in to the exercise:

Intention – You honestly want to forgive and move on from this issue.

Compassion – You genuinely wish to relieve the suffering for yourself and those involved.

It is now time for you to liberate and free yourself.

You may be feeling apprehensive, it's natural.

You have spent your life believing that forgiveness is a difficult option.

That this stuff has to stay with us.

Once you have gone through this exercise a few times and realised its life-changing benefits, your apprehension will quickly be replaced by an eagerness to do the work.

I have included an illustrated example at the end of each section to assist you with each exercise.

"Forgiving yourself"

Take a plain piece of paper and at the top of the page in the centre I would like you to write your own name within inverted commas.

Below your name, again in inverted commas write the reason or the issue that requires your forgiveness, look to simplify this to a phrase or short sentence.

Now in the centre of the page draw a big heart, for most of us the image of a heart signifies love and compassion and therefore contains the contents in a safe and supportive space.

Within the heart begin to write down words or phrases that explain possible reasons that may have caused this issue.

Go easy on yourself, this is an opportunity for you to gently go beyond your actions and explore what may have brought them about.

Simply write down anything that comes to you, no matter how irrelevant it may seem.

Once you feel that you have exhausted the process take a few moments to review what you have placed within your heart.

One word or phrase will usually begin to grow stronger, it may have meant very little when written but will now appear to make the others seem less significant.

Focus on the chosen word or words, perhaps draw a line around them, more often than not this will be the underlying cause of your discomfort.

Now begin to understand that this one reason has been at the root of your unease, you have suffered enough and it is time to let it go.

It is now time for you to affirm your act of forgiveness, to truly release yourself from whatever was attaching you to the subject so you can finally free yourself from it.

Look again at the page, you should be proud of what you have achieved, you have taken something that was buried and faced it, you have made a commitment to yourself and to the universe that enough is enough and it's time to move on.

As you review your work, begin to feel a sense of gratitude and relief, quietly give thanks that the time has finally come to forgive.

Count your blessings, take your pen and write at the bottom of the page in the centre and again in inverted comma's "I forgive you."

Finally, with gratitude, an increasing sense of relief and from your heart, say I forgive you together with your own name slowly three times.

"Sam"

"I'm dishonest"

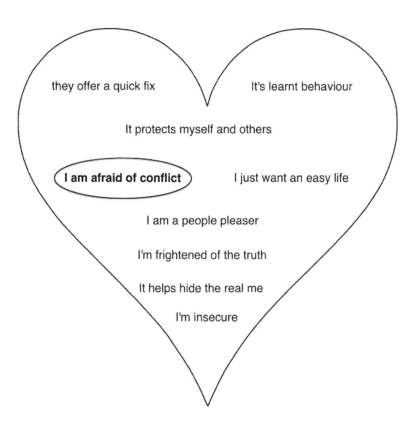

they offer a quick fix

It's learnt behaviour

It protects myself and others

I am afraid of conflict

I just want an easy life

I am a people pleaser

I'm frightened of the truth

It helps hide the real me

I'm insecure

"I forgive you Sam"

"Forgiving others"

As with the self-forgiveness exercise take a plain piece of paper.

At the top of the page in the centre I would like you to write the name of the person who you wish to forgive, place the name within inverted commas.

Below the name, again in inverted commas write the reason or the issue that requires your forgiveness, look to simplify this to a phrase or short sentence.

Before you begin ask yourself the following:

Have I ever done this?

Have I ever considered or been responsible for a similar action or situation for which I now hold another guilty?

Be honest with yourself as this is a significant part of the forgiveness process.

This question alone will dilute the effect of the issue that you are working on.

Next, as with the self-forgiveness exercise, draw a big heart in the middle of the page.

Now I would like you to draw a horizontal line within your heart, so you divide it in half from left to right.

In the bottom half, begin to look at reasons why this person may have acted this way, look beyond the act; that has gone forever.

Allow yourself to acknowledge that this isn't the person's true nature and on some level they will have acted out of fear.

Be absolute in the knowledge that their true self would never have wished you any harm.

Write within the segment simple phrases or words that begin to help you understand why this took place.

Now working above the line within your heart, I would like you to think about how this process that you have initiated will benefit you.

What will your compassion bring to you? What effect will your simple, virtuous act have on you as you move forward in life, and write it down.

For this particular section you may wish to keep your writing a little smaller as there's a lot to cram in!

When complete, take a moment to look at the page.

At the top in the centre is the name of the person who you wish to forgive, just below you have written the issue or reason for you taking the time to work through this.

Below that you have your big heart, once empty but now full.

It is now time for you to affirm your act of forgiveness, to truly release yourself from whatever was attaching you to the subject so you can finally free yourself from it.

Look at the page, once again you should be proud of what you have achieved, you have taken something that was buried and faced it, you have made a commitment to yourself and to the universe that enough is enough and it's time to move on.

As you review your work, begin to feel a sense of gratitude and relief, quietly give thanks that the time has finally come to forgive.

Count your blessings, take your pen and write at the bottom of the page in the centre and again in inverted commas "I forgive you."

Finally, with gratitude, an increasing sense of relief and from your heart say I forgive you together with the name of the person slowly three times.

There is a wonderful knock on effect to this approach to forgiveness.

Even though the other person may have no idea of your intention, their higher or inner self does.

Very often you will notice a positive shift in your relationship or whenever you interact with them.

I have many examples of how the other person's approach to me "seemingly" changed for the better after I had chosen to release myself from a negative connection to them.

Forgiveness enables you to once again look at people in a positive light, and as we get back what we give out, so will they.

"My boss"

"She doesn't appreciate me"

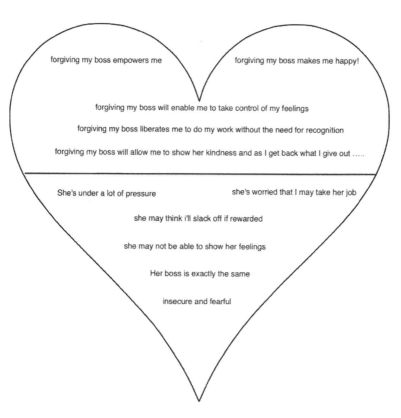

forgiving my boss empowers me

forgiving my boss makes me happy!

forgiving my boss will enable me to take control of my feelings

forgiving my boss liberates me to do my work without the need for recognition

forgiving my boss will allow me to show her kindness and as I get back what I give out .....

She's under a lot of pressure

she's worried that I may take her job

she may think i'll slack off if rewarded

she may not be able to show her feelings

Her boss is exactly the same

insecure and fearful

"I forgive you"

"Evening Reflection"

In every moment your life brings to you endless opportunities to offer a kind, caring approach towards yourself and others.

Take time at the end of each day to revisit your three morning kindness affirmations, change them slightly in order for you to reflect on how your day went.

Just for Today did I show a random act of kindness to a stranger and tell no one?

Just for Today was I able to look for opportunities to help another person unconditionally and expect nothing in return?

Just for Today have I gone easy on my supposed faults choosing to focus instead on what I have done for others?

Quite often in those quiet moments just after we awake or before we go to sleep we let our ego mind take over and we start and finish our day worried or anxious.

Just a few minutes spent with the above each day enables you to fall asleep at peace and safe in the knowledge that when you awake your early morning thoughts will be kind and compassionate.

A guided meditation to develop Forgiveness.

A short guided meditation that will further enhance this chapter can be found at www.iantucker.co.uk

Gratitude

"If the only prayer you say in your
entire life is thank you, it will
be enough."

As we begin to recognise the life-changing benefits of forgiveness and build it into our everyday lives it will lessen the hold that past events have on us, and in turn help us to let go of emotions such as grief and regret.

It will enable us to feel more present and by not remaining stuck in the past, we have so much more energy to enjoy today.

But what of the future?

Just as you arrive eager to live in this moment someone reminds you of the total uncertainty of tomorrow.

How can we then stop ourselves finally stepping out of the past only to let our minds wander to future events where worry, anxiety and uncertainty replace regret?

As the pace of life takes hold of us we are swept along with the belief that we need more to be happy, that what we already have isn't enough.

We become dependent on something or someone coming along in the future that will make it all perfect.

It's at this point that we introduce the need to control an outcome, or feel helpless because we can't. Thus opening the door to heartache and damaging thoughts associated with worry, apprehension and fear.

What if we allowed ourselves to stop for a moment, and acknowledge all the good that we have in our life? To focus on what we have rather than what we think we need?

What if we simply said thank you?

If someone told you that at this point in your life you were to draw a line and have nothing more than you have now, you would quickly rediscover, learn to value and cherish how blessed you already are.

Being grateful refocuses us on the moment. It eases our concerns about what might have been or indeed what may or may not come along in the future. It helps us to recognise all that we have NOW.

Gratitude is a true healing balm for the modern age. It gently soothes the pain of needing more to be happy whilst softening the effect of regret for something in the past.

As forgiveness sets you free and delivers you to this moment, gratitude takes over and offers a reminder of how fortunate you are right now.

The combination of forgiveness and gratitude are an unbeatable force. Later in this chapter I will introduce you to a simple approach that will enable you to work through a situation and find peace and inspiration when previously you may have given up all hope.

You need very little in life to be truly happy and at peace, in fact the real irony is that the more you have, the more you think you need.

Stuck on the side of the refrigerator your happy and "at peace" list would only read food, water, shelter, health and loving interaction with other people.

You may feel that even this eludes you, food, water and shelter are normally in stock but the health and loving other people bit isn't always available.

I guess that you can probably imagine what the effect of not worrying about the future would have on your general well-being.

You can also be assured that as you shift towards a more simple, caring outlook to life, as you begin to develop a compassionate, giving nature, an inner glow will begin to radiate from you.

The very essence of these qualities is love itself and it will naturally attract other people into your life, and as you always get back what you give out, the final item on your list is also in place.

The magical thing about giving thanks is that nothing has to change in your life. The circumstances remain the same. Just like forgiveness your ability to be grateful every day does not depend on anyone or anything else.

So what stops us? Why do we seemingly forget all that we have? Why are loved ones and dear friends taken for granted?

What makes it so difficult for us to count our blessings?

Our need for always wanting more brings with it a dissatisfaction for what we believe we have right now. This leads us to blame others for our supposed shortfalls and brings a pessimistic outlook.

We begin to complain. To whinge. To whine. To criticise, and before we know it our self-pity has stifled any chance we have of allowing us to remain positive.

Complaint is the direct opposite of gratitude. One liberates whilst the other suffocates. One empowers you to recognise all that you have. The other is born out of a self-righteous belief that the world isn't meeting your expectations and needs to do better.

A law that runs through this book just as it does throughout your life is the principle of what you give out you get back.

Another approach to this would be that what you focus on expands. It fills your mind, becomes your truth and turns into your reality

Therefore, if what we put our attention on becomes our story, our life, you can begin to see how damaging complaint and self-pity can be.

Complaining simply brings more into your life for you to complain about!

The great news is that the same law also applies to gratitude.

As you begin to give thanks and show appreciation for all that you have in life, even more of the same presents itself to you.

Within no time at all and just by changing your approach from scarcity to abundance you will quickly develop a more positive and realistic outlook on life.

Let's now look at how we can create this internal shift each day.

I have already mentioned that you have everything you need to be grateful right now.

Therefore, a perfect place to start is to look at things that we currently take for granted.

Those people or things in your life that have become background noise. An inconvenience to you in your quest to find more and thus be happy. The older model. The "hold you back" brigade.

The people closest to us in our life offer us an ideal opportunity to reignite our appreciation for all that we have.

Why is it that even though there is a very good chance that we would give our own life to keep these people safe, we still find it easy to criticise and complain rather than remember how blessed we are that they are sharing our life?

The very fact that we spend more time with them means that they come with a workload. They are demanding of us and take up more of our time, and in turn our expectation of them also increases.

Real life kicks in and your day to day routine takes over.

The school run. Shopping. Cooking. Cleaning. The pressures of work. Family issues. Finances. Health. You will all have your own list, but you get the picture.

As it rises to the surface we get dragged along with it and it becomes our reality. The problem is it also becomes the people with whom you share it, and that's what brings the negativity towards them and vice versa.

Gratitude takes you below the surface, it enables you to look past the monotony and reconnect with the person rather than the "to do" list.

It moves you out of self-pity and reminds you how blessed you are.

You can find a hundred reasons to love someone, for every one reason to complain, and guess what comes back to you?

So as we begin to understand the art of appreciation, can we relate it to all things, however basic? Or does there need to be a value or importance placed on an item before we can truly give thanks?

My writing space is a small woodshed in South Devon, England.

It has a log burner and a desk. It really couldn't be any more basic.

It has no obvious monetary value and I could have been put off by the buckets that catch the rainwater from a leaking roof.

Yet I have developed a deep sense of gratitude for this place.

On the surface it's small. It leaks. It has no real insulation. Its approach is down an often ridiculously muddy track. It has a growing wasp problem, and a family of ducks sometimes choose to quack away outside the door. Finally, I share it with some of the biggest spiders I've ever seen.

My appreciation takes me below the surface. The desk is uncluttered and sits against a large window that overlooks a beautiful tranquil meadow.

At the top of the meadow an oak tree offers shade, and at certain times of the day the light weaves its way through the branches bringing warmth as it bathes the room.

If I arrive early a mist hangs on the stillness and offers a beautiful serene quality.

The silence is occasionally broken by the chorus of birdsong, and even as I write a squirrel chases along the window sill and across the floor before returning to the oak.

I have developed a wasp exit plan to be proud of, and have come to love the quacking and waddling of the ducks, and even though I say it myself I think it's mutual.

So you see the situation is exactly the same; it's simply what you choose to focus on, the bucket or the view.

Gratitude changes your life.

Literally!

It is as if the universe acknowledges that you now recognise all that you have and delivers even more to you. It's a self-fulfilling prophecy.

When I set out to write this book I knew that I would need the assistance of both a musician and an artist.

Even though I hadn't begun writing I felt that by incorporating images and spoken words the message would resonate with more people.

I had recently recorded a guided meditation for another project and although I had only ever used it within my workshops it was well received.

I awoke one morning with the idea of offering it to a select number of online music websites.

I sat at my computer, searched the internet and subsequently sent about 30 emails.

I only ever received one reply and it was within half an hour.

My phone rang and a gentleman introduced himself as Paul, we began to speak and he mentioned that besides running the website he was also a professional musician who specialised in music to aid meditation and relaxation.

As we were on the phone I began listening to sample tracks from his website. Within 30 seconds I knew that I had found the perfect piece for Your Simple Path.

As I put the phone down it took a while to sink in. I knew that I had wanted to find a musician but had no idea how, and ideally someone who would have empathy with the book and what I wanted to achieve.

Within an hour I had met someone, found the perfect track and he loved the idea of the book.

I felt a tremendous wave of appreciation, not just a thank you, it was more than that.

I knew that somehow our paths were meant to cross and for that I felt a deep sense of gratitude.

A few days later and I again woke up with the book on my mind. This time it was a feeling that I should find somewhere quiet, somewhere inspirational to make a start, to bring the idea to life.

During a recent family visit to Cornwall we had found a beautiful beach attached to a small village.

The day had been perfect and my wife and I both agreed we should find a way of spending more time there.

So I decided to look into renting a very simple space there for a few days, to be near the ocean and think about the book.

I again found myself at the computer. This time searching for room or studio space for hire in the same village and close to the beach.

My search took me to someone who had a room in the village. I began the email to ask if it would be available to rent but then noticed that it was her own studio where she displayed her paintings.

She was an artist whose approach to creating her work was again very much in tune with the book's message.

One email and a wonderful phone call was all it took and just like Paul, Annie B was on board.

I have an absolute belief that my heartfelt gratitude at finding Paul and the music had a big part to play in me searching for a room to hire in a small remote Cornish village.

What could have been a global, exhaustive search had introduced two like-minded souls to me within a few days of having the initial idea.

So count your blessings, and as you begin to focus on all that you have in your life you can expect thoughts of lack and scarcity to disappear.

You will not only become mindful of all that you already have but also attract more into your life.

There is a wonderful irony to developing a grateful outlook on life, perfectly summarised by bestselling author Eckhart Tolle:

If you want abundance, you need to find that sense of fullness first, which is inseparable from the present moment.

"Developing Gratitude in your
everyday Life."

"Morning Gratitude"

"Give Thanks"

"Restful Contemplation"

"Morning Gratitude"

Begin each day with a simple practice of morning gratitude.

Many of us will wake up and use this quiet time to think about our day ahead, and this can often be a time when any issues or worries arise.

This quick and easy practice takes just a few minutes each morning and will allow you to counteract negative thoughts and replace them with all you have to be thankful for as you start your day.

Take a few moments to clear your mind.

Now think of someone or something in your life that makes you smile, you may not even have met them, but you are grateful that you know them.

I would like you to look to change the focus of your first smile each morning.

Now expand this a little and begin to think of other things in your life that you are grateful for, just a few to start your day on the right footing.

Look to subtly change them each morning and if for whatever reason it just doesn't flow then go back to basics.

For example:

Do you step out of your warm bed onto soft carpet?
Will the tap produce clean flowing water at a single turn?
Does the morning sun gently bathe your room?
Are you free to offer someone a caring, genuine smile today?

This time spent each morning whilst allowing and encouraging yourself to realise all that you have in life won't just brighten your day.

It will change your life.

"Give Thanks"

At any point during your day you can use this uplifting exercise to focus on a specific person (including yourself) or subject that you wish to give or develop gratitude for.

As with the forgiveness "within your heart" exercise take a plain piece of paper.

Now write "Thank You and a name or word" in inverted commas at the top of the page.

Draw your heart in the centre of the page, and write the person's name or simple phrase inside it.

Clear your mind and look to nurture a feeling of appreciation.

Now begin to find things that you are thankful for associated with what you have placed "within your heart" and write them down as they come to you.

Fill the page around your heart and prepare to amaze yourself. Gratitude flows as a result of you simply focusing on what was there all along.

There is a real depth to this work, you could choose any initial reason to be grateful and literally fill another page with that as the focus within the heart.

This inspiring and yet very simple exercise not only helps you to give thanks for things that come easily to you. It will also bring clarity and reduce stress with people or issues that occasionally come along and test you in life.

It will help you to realise that we can all find things to appreciate in any situation that comes our way.

On the following page is an illustrated example, for this I have chosen our beautiful dog Flo.

"Thank you Flo"

She's so funny without even knowing it.
She accepts me totally, always there for me.
She's like sunshine.
Loves me.
Makes us laugh.

Our dog Flo x

Opens my heart.
Helps me make friends. Keeps me fit. She gets me out
in the rain.
She has caring eyes, keeps me warm.
She's unconditional, protective, she's calming.

"Restful Contemplation"

However hectic or busy your day has been you usually have time at the end of it to reflect on how it has gone.

This is another ideal opportunity to focus on finding positive elements within any situation.

Begin with things that have happened that bring a smile to your face.

As you relax, recognise that warm, happy sensation at your ability to feel gratitude that this person or event has become part of your life.

Every day things will also come along to test us in some way. It normally suggests that something or someone hasn't quite met our expectations or the outcome isn't how we had envisaged it would be.

However, please keep in mind that very often we end up relieved that things didn't progress as we had hoped and are even more grateful for a completely different outcome.

As you take a moment at the end of the day to reflect on such things, look to develop a gentle understanding that there is an opportunity to learn and grow from everything that comes into our lives and that such fortune enables us to become a better, happier and more grounded person.

This simple practice just before you go to sleep each evening will help you finish your day in a calm, peaceful and reflective frame of mind.

A guided meditation to develop Gratitude.

A short guided meditation that will further enhance this chapter can be found at www.iantucker.co.uk

"Forgiveness and Gratitude."

"A formidable force."

The previous two chapters have unveiled to you not only the absolute benefits of forgiveness and gratitude, but also introduced a number of simple yet powerful exercises that follow a similar approach.

You are encouraged to begin and finish each day with a gentle focus on appreciating all that you have, whilst looking for opportunities to show and practice a compassionate outlook towards yourself and others.

Just those few minutes spent each day alone will have an amazingly positive effect on how you feel and approach life's journey.

They will create a subtle yet exciting shift within you, as compassion sets your intention on what you can do for others whilst lessening your expectation of what life owes you.

At the same time helping you to finally realise how fortunate you are reduces your need for always wanting more.

Each chapter also offers you an opportunity to develop forgiveness and gratitude at any time of the day towards a specific subject.

Until this point you will have used them in isolation, but combined they have a tremendous potential to bring peace to any situation.

In this wonderfully simple but liberating exercise you gently allow your compassionate approach to the person or situation to cleanse and remove your negative thoughts and emotions that have been attached to it.

This then creates a space for you to actually find the gift that is available to you in every situation.

Using the illustration that follows allow me to show you how combining the two will create an amazingly liberating effect on your well-being.

At the top of the page in inverted commas write the person's name you wish to forgive.

As with the previous exercises draw a heart on your page, and make a horizontal line through it's centre.

Working below the line, revisit how your forgiveness will benefit you, a wonderful reminder that you don't have to hold on.

Once you feel that this is complete write "I forgive you" at the bottom of the page.

Let above the line become a realisation that there is a blessing, something to give thanks for in every situation and let your pen flow in gratitude.

Once you have finished simply write "Thank you" below the person's name.

And it is done, in a short space of time you have taken something that weakened you, and worked through it to liberate and empower yourself to move on from it.

"My boss"

I am grateful that everyone is different

I am grateful to my boss for the lesson

I am grateful that I have learned the importance of rewarding and motivating others

I am grateful for the oportunity to grow and develop my personal skills

I am grateful for my job and all that it brings to me

forgiving my boss will allow me to show her kindness and as I get back wat I give out .....

forgiving my boss liberates me to do my work without the need for recognition

forgiving my boss will enable me to take control of my feelings

forgiving my boss makes me happy!

forgiving my boss empowers me

"Thank you"

"I forgive you"

Peace

"How at Peace you feel is your true
measure of success in life."

Every word written within this book is with the intention of you finding peace within your life.

To help you recognise and nurture an inner calm that money, success or material possession just can't buy.

A way of life that doesn't see your happiness tied to an outcome or dependent upon something that will only end up gathering dust or thrown out.

A simple understanding that you already have everything you need to be happy and that a relentless search for more will only take you further away from it.

There is no need to go looking for peace as it will find you.

The first thing to do is less.

But what about the go getters? The over achievers? The life and soul of the party types? What happens if you work twenty-four seven? Lead from the front? Win at all costs?

Could you snooze and still not lose? Is working twenty-three seven such a failure? Can less really be more?

To be at peace you need to find balance.

Balance brings with it breathing space, a space to breathe, to just be.

This breathing space is different. It isn't just a diluted extension of your day, where you replay all that's going on in your life.

It isn't half an hour in front of the television or chatting on the phone.

It offers you the chance to free yourself from "day to day" and reconnect with a part of you that has sat quietly and waited.

Our first step towards reacquaintance with this inner, peaceful self is to build silence into our day.

For many of us this will be the first time in our life that we have become silent. We wake up to the sound of an alarm and from that moment noise fills our heads.

All day. Every day. If we walk into a quiet room we switch something on. If we get into a car we switch something on. Shops, elevators, restaurants all switch something on, and now our white noise comes with headphones for added intensity.

Finding a period of silence each day will become as much a part of Your Simple Path to happiness as anything else that you have read in this book.

I'm not suggesting you become a hermit or take a vow here, just a few minutes each day when you make a commitment to yourself that you will become silent.

It's good to arrange a space within your home that you automatically associate with this quiet time. But it's not a necessity, if like me you have a young family then this can be difficult.

My inspiration for this book and indeed much of its content was born out of periods of silence as I walked my dog in a nearby wood.

Sometimes, however, this has been replaced by a hotel room, a car journey, a waiting room, a walk across town, it's more about your intent than your surroundings.

Initially, our ego will jump at the chance to sabotage this perfect opportunity and look to fill your space with triviality and reasons to go and switch something on.

But with a little perseverance something very interesting begins to happen. Your ego's chatter falls silent and is gently replaced.

It's as if a veil has been slowly lifted, and your true light, your real voice, is released.

For many it will be the first time in your life that you have experienced true peace. It may only last a few seconds at first. But will be enough for you to understand that there is a way out of the worry and anxiety.

And after a lifetime of looking outside of yourself for answers they were just a few deep breaths away all along.

I once read a line from the Persian poet Rumi, who wrote "Out beyond ideas of wrongdoing and rightdoing, there is a field, I'll see you there."

This wonderfully tranquil place, this feeling, is only ever a few minutes in silence away from however your day is going.

At first it will offer us respite. A place to dwell away from the noise. However, very soon and with a little practise we begin to develop a connection, a bond that will last forever.

You see every answer you ever need will be found in your own silence, and it will always bring you happiness.

It will show you a kind and balanced solution every time as it emanates from a place that only knows peace, compassion and understanding.

Our inner self knows the big picture. It holds our life story, our reason for being here, our purpose, and silence is the key that opens the door.

It has watched as we chose again and again to act out of fear for some narrow-minded quick fix.

Remained resolute as we were helplessly blown around like a leaf in the wind clinging onto what we thought we needed.

It has waited patiently for Love's Whisper to gently call your name.

And as you stop running for your life and catch your breath it will reveal to you everything that you ever needed.

So what is the next step after identifying the importance of silence in our search for inner peace?

We must develop a trust in what emerges, and as we remain open will begin to understand how the universe really works, and in time, who we really are.

To quote Martin Luther King, Jr.: "Faith means taking the first step even when you don't see the whole staircase."

As the relationship unfolds and we begin to look for guidance there will be times when we have to trust our inner feelings, even if they conflict with what seems like a logical decision.

This is because our ego creates a fearful, short-term, immediate approach. Where we act in an attempt to control an outcome based only on what we can see, what we think we know or even what's in it for us.

But remember that your inner or true self, your source of wisdom will guide you in line with your highest good, your "bigger picture" every time.

As we become silent and look for guidance it will reveal itself in different ways.

For me the message comes as a feeling, but it could be visual such as pictures or written words, it may be audible, but always kind.

Sometimes significant, often subtle, but always kind.

A kind approach brings you peace every time, there is no conflict in kindness, no losers, no ego.

Can you see how this begins to take shape?

Once you get past your ego and re-establish a relationship with your true wisdom you will bring a flow into your life that will amaze you.

Your mind, so full of damaging and limiting thoughts is set free. You are re-energized as negative emotions that for so long have weighed you down disappear along with your ego's stranglehold on how you should or shouldn't live your life.

Instead of your ego's limiting beliefs, hidden talents are revealed to you that enable you to approach life with a quiet yet exhilarating confidence.

And because at last you are now living the life that was meant for you the universe will bring things onto your path that will enhance not only your life, but that of others too.

The right person will show up (or indeed disappear from your life) at just the right time. Doors open. Opportunities present themselves, and why wouldn't they?

The world's been waiting for you.

Let me give you a personal example.

For a few years I had been running workshops and courses on various subjects ranging from a holistic approach to well-being to recognising spirituality within the healthcare sector and lots in between.

In 2011 I was invited to do some work for a company owned by a close friend of mine. He had offered me a very generous salary and my role was to join the company and develop a new strategic focus.

The U.K. was right in the middle of the biggest economic downturn in its history. Every day brought more news of redundancy and companies having to close.

So as you can imagine the income and job security came at the perfect time for me and my family, or so I thought.

As I sat in silence one day, I got an emerging but overwhelming feeling that I was going to write a book, this book.

Within minutes I knew its name and had even sketched the front cover (possibly the first time in twenty years that I had attempted to draw anything).

I also developed an understanding that in order for me to be able to give it my full attention something would have to give, and that something was the day job.

My ego immediately began to list all the reasons why this couldn't possibly work, for a start I wasn't a writer, I mean that's quite a big one.

I'm too busy at work. I'll have no money. I have a mortgage.

How will I support my family? What if I can't do it? What if I can but it doesn't get published?

Unfortunately for my ego I had already read the Martin Luther King quote.

On the day that I decided to tell my friend and company owner of my decision I sat in the reception and watched the lunchtime news on the flat screen TV.

It was so full of economic doom, gloom and disaster that it made what I was about to do seem ridiculous.

That day I took the first step, and kept walking, and here's what is so fantastic about keeping the faith.

Once you make the commitment, once you say to the universe "OK, I've listened and I'm in – I'm going to do it."

The people show up, the doors open, and the opportunities present themselves.

What's all this got to do with finding peace?

Well, just like choosing kindness, being true to yourself brings peace every time.

So through silence and a little faith, find your own inner peace and inspire others to do the same.

"I choose Peace every time"

The following page offers you a blueprint that will bring peace to any situation.

I would ask you to take everything that you have read so far into this exercise with you.

If it made sense to you as you read it then here is your opportunity to bring it into your life and find a peaceful solution.

So. Are you able to approach the following page from a position of simply wanting to be happy?

Can you remove your ego's desire to win or control the situation and be at peace?

Do you see the benefit of letting go and moving on?

As in previous chapters start with minor issues as you look to develop a peaceful approach to everyday life.

To conclude this chapter I encourage you to listen to the guided meditation called Peace that can be found at www.iantucker.co.uk

It will assist you in developing a better understanding whilst also introducing you to the connection with your inner or true Self.

"Developing Peace into your
Everyday Life"

"Every single choice I make will either
enhance my spirit or drain my spirit, there
is nothing in between."

"Does my reaction to this issue bring
me Peace?"

"I choose Peace every time."

Freedom

"Be true to yourself, Be Free."

As you step onto Your Simple Path travel light.

Look to reduce your excess baggage.

You won't require worry or regret for the journey, they only ever weighed you down when you did pack them.

There's no need for leaving space either as you will be looking to give rather than take from now on.

Don't concern yourself with having to plan every turn before you set out as each step will reveal where you go next and your inner guidance system will take you to exactly where you need to be.

Others may come to you for directions but just let them know what they need to pack and wish them well.

You can't tell them the way as there is no destination. Each step is the journey, and so we only need to find happiness in each step.

In your bag you need just a few essentials to help you along your way.

Forgiveness will keep you looking forward and put a spring in your step.

Gratitude will help you to realise just how lucky you are to be in these shoes.

And so to inner peace, and with it the greatest gift of all – Freedom.

A freedom that has no reliance upon any external factors.

No attachment to anyone or anything that may appear or disappear from your life.

A personal freedom that emanates from understanding what really matters in life and living it.

You're free. You always were but now you know it.

And by example you are also free to liberate others and help them to step onto their Simple Path.

Life

Life – it's a simple word. In essence it's the period between birth and death, most of us get about eighty years at it and are generally provided with everything that we need to have a good time.

They even tell us that the best things in life are free and so on paper we have it made.

Common sense would suggest that if we spend eighty years doing something we'd become pretty good at it, but for some reason, that doesn't seem the case with life.

As you read this book you're living your life.

How's it going? No, seriously, how's it going?

You are the perfect age to bring peace and happiness into your life.

The title or label others choose for you is nothing more than a recognition of your life experience to this point.

You have come to understand that a few letters arranged on a business card don't define you. Only you can define you.

At this very moment whether you are relaxing on a sofa, dug in on a battlefield, commuting on a packed train or waiting on death row, you are free. A freedom that is an internal choice and not reliant upon external factors.

Your natural beauty radiates from within, born out of a kind, caring compassionate approach to life and others.

It shines brighter and makes you far more attractive than any skin deep, quick fix formula.

You may have wanted to look different, but now only look forward to picking the perfect nose without the need to change its shape.

There have been times in your life when your happiness was

dependent upon something outside of your control.

You now see the frailty of this and choose to be at peace with all that you have right now.

This is in the knowledge that as you do less, you get more. In slowing down and focusing on all that you have in life, more finds its way to you.

You are able to recognise that judgment and criticism stem from insecurity and fear. A compassionate approach helps you to look past the empty words and move on each time.

You live in a world that works day and night to make you just like everyone else. Don't fit in. Wear what makes you feel good. Eat what you like. Be comfortable in your skin and you will inspire others to do the same.

It seems that Society has a plan for all of us and you have a part to play.

Choose your own part and don't leave it to someone else.

Set out to win. Give it everything and look to inspire and motivate others. But play fair and always with respect. True quality shows through as much in defeat as victory.

What will the children in your life remember when they think of you?

Your kind, caring nature will stay with them for a lifetime. Whilst making sure they have the latest model only lasts as long as the latest model.

Living your dreams reduces your debt. Do what you love and the money will follow.

As your outlook on life changes so will the people who are in it. Their attraction to you will be based upon who you are and not what you have.

In turn, you now notice people for what's in their hearts rather than their bank accounts.

Friendships born this way last a lifetime.

Are you the person the world expects you to be or the person you really want to be?

Only one of these brings health and happiness.

Nothing energises you like being true to who you really are.

Silence brings meaning and with it every answer that you will ever need.

As you develop an understanding and connection with this inner self it offers peace to you in every situation.

It only ever delivers kindness, compassion and understanding.

All religions offer us a lifetime of learning in the hope of finding this place, and many do.

Let silence and a little trust take you there without having to open the manual.

So, as you come to the end of this book, what are the moments that really matter and do you make the most of them?

Will you simply exist and react to your life or can you make more of a difference?

Do you live the life that you want for yourself or the one others expect of you?

Finally, and perhaps the most poignant reflection asks what is your life for?

Does your life have purpose?

Because now, it has meaning.

"Do you take care of me?"

It is now the end of your first day at school and through the window you can see that everyone apart from you has left the class.

You watch as "little you" packs your bag and misbuttons your coat.

Suddenly they look up and you both smile exactly the same smile.

As you walk slowly into the classroom they sit down and you take the small chair next to them.

They reach for your hand and look up into your eyes, you will know exactly how they are feeling.

"How am I?" they ask nervously.

"You're fine, you're doing great," you reply warmly with a smile.

"I am?" they say excitedly, a picture of innocence. "Do you take care of me?"

"Yes I do, I take real good care of you."

"Am I happy?" they ask now a little tearful.

"Yes, you are, you're very happy."

"What makes me happy?" they ask smiling as a single tear rolls down their cheek.

You smile back gently as you hand them a tissue.

"Little things make you happy, like thinking about how lucky you are to have everything that you have in life."

"Why is that so important?"

"Well, it helps you to stop worrying about the future because you have so much to be thankful for already."

"Do I have all that I need to be happy?"

"We all do, it's just that some people choose to concentrate on all the things they don't have, but happy people understand it."

"What else makes me happy?" they ask.

"Well, making other people smile makes you smile too, and giving things to your friends or someone who needs it more than you, now that makes you really happy."

"Well, that sounds easy."

"It is easy but lots of people forget and think being happy depends on what they can get from others."

"So I just have to be kind then?" they say with a smile.

"I guess so, you don't need much more because whatever you do for others they will want to give back to you, so yes simply being kind brings happiness every time."

It's time for little you to leave class for today, you remain seated so as they stand you are both at eye level.

Looking into your eyes they step forward and hold you close.

"Thank you," they whisper. "For taking care of me."

"You're welcome," you reply, "and when you come into school tomorrow, be sure to remember the golden rules, because as our teacher said, they are for life."

Do you take care of me?

Just for today

Were you honest?

Did you worry about things?

Were you kind to everyone that you met?

Have you lost your temper and got angry with people?

Did you remember what you already have in life to make you happy?

"All is well"

"Should I worry about what ifs or feel regret about
the past?

Let anxiety prevail in case this moment doesn't last,

Or can I relax, feel safe and know that everything
is fine,

And let serenity and peace guide me through
every time."

Your Simple Path

Find Happiness in every step

Ian Tucker

www.iantucker.co.uk

BOOKS

O is a symbol of the world, of oneness and unity. In different cultures it also means the "eye," symbolizing knowledge and insight. We aim to publish books that are accessible, constructive and that challenge accepted opinion, both that of academia and the "moral majority."

Our books are available in all good English language bookstores worldwide. If you don't see the book on the shelves ask the bookstore to order it for you, quoting the ISBN number and title. Alternatively you can order online (all major online retail sites carry our titles) or contact the distributor in the relevant country, listed on the copyright page.

See our website **www.o-books.net** for a full list of over 500 titles, growing by 100 a year.

And tune in to myspiritradio.com for our book review radio show, hosted by June-Elleni Laine, where you can listen to the authors discussing their books.